Machines at Work
Bulldozers

by Cari Meister

Bullfrog Books

Ideas for Parents and Teachers

Bullfrog Books let children practice nonfiction reading at the earliest reading levels. Repetition, familiar words, and photo labels support early readers.

Before Reading
- Discuss the cover photo. What does it tell them?
- Look at the picture glossary together. Read and discuss the words.

Read the Book
- "Walk" through the book and look at the photos. Let the child ask questions. Point out the photo labels.
- Read the book to the child, or have him or her read independently.

After Reading
- Prompt the child to think more. Ask: Have you ever seen a bulldozer? What was it doing?

Bullfrog Books are published by Jump!
5357 Penn Avenue South
Minneapolis, MN 55419
www.jumplibrary.com

Library of Congress Cataloging-in-Publication Data
Meister, Cari.
  Bulldozers / by Cari Meister.
    pages cm. -- (Bullfrog books. Machines at work)
  Includes bibliographical references and index.
  Summary: "This photo-illustrated book for early readers tells about the parts of a bulldozer and how people use bulldozers in construction"-- Provided by publisher.
  Audience: Age 5.
  Audience: Grades K to grade 3.
  ISBN 978-1-62031-044-1 (hardcover : alk. paper) -- ISBN 978-1-62496-056-7 (ebook)
  1. Bulldozers--Juvenile literature. 2. Earthwork--Juvenile literature. I. Title.
  TA725.M37 2014
  629.225--dc23   2012042016

Series designer: Ellen Huber
Book designer: Sara Pokorny
Photo Researcher: Heather Dreisbach

Photo Credits:
123RF, 11, 18, 23br; Alamy, 9, 13, 17, 21; Corbis, 14; Getty, 23tl; Shutterstock, cover, 1, 3, 4, 5, 6, 7, 10, 12, 15, 22, 23bl, 23tr, 24

Printed in the United States of America at Corporate Graphics in North Mankato, Minnesota.
5-2013 / PO 1003

10 9 8 7 6 5 4 3 2 1

Table of Contents

A Bulldozer at Work

What is clearing the path?

A bulldozer!

How does it work?

Look at the sharp ripper.
It breaks up hard clay.

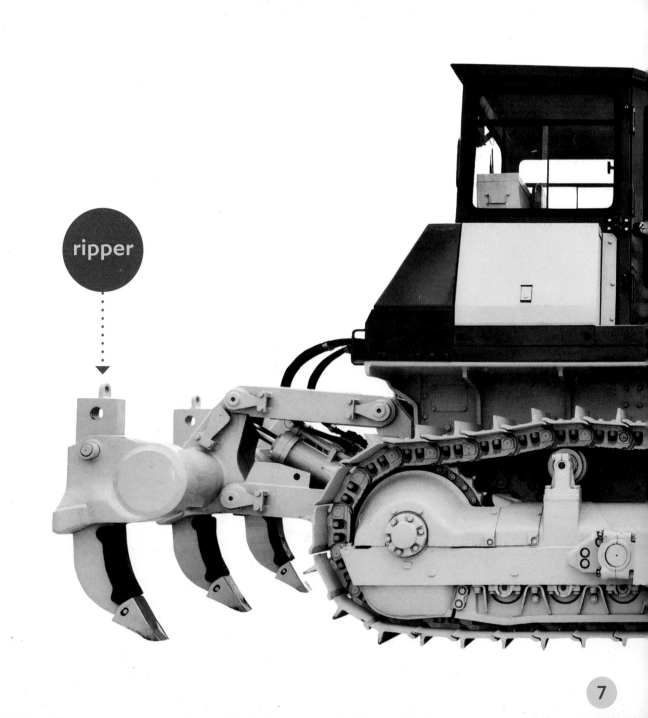

ripper

Look at the
heavy blade.

It pushes dirt.

blade

Look at the bumpy tracks.
They keep the bulldozer
from sinking.

tracks ● ● ● ● ● ● ● ● ▶

The driver sits
in the cab.

It is loud.

She has
ear muffs.

Beep! Beep!

She backs up.

14

The ground is flat.

Now a road can be built.

What more do
they do?

They make
paths in woods.

Smash! Crash!

They move rocks in quarries.

Rumble. Tumble.

Oh no!
An avalanche!

Push. Plow.

Now the cars can go.

Parts of a Bulldozer

cab
The part of the bulldozer where the driver sits.

blade
A heavy part on the front of a bulldozer that can go up and down.

D11R

ripper
An extra part of a bulldozer that can tear a deep, narrow hole in the ground.

tracks
Wide, heavy metal links that give a bulldozer good traction.